Unveiling the Truth about the War in the Womb

Dr. Aaron B. Claxton, PhD

Kingdom Publishing LLC
1350 Blair Drive
Odenton, MD 21113
Printed in the USA

Unveiling the Truth about the War in the Womb

Copyright © 2017 by Dr. Aaron B. Claxton, PhD

All rights reserved. No part of this book may be reproduced or transmitted in any form or by any means without written permission of the author.

Scripture quotations marked KJV are taken from the Holy Bible, King James Version (Public Domain). Scripture quotations marked YLT are taken from The Young's Literal Translation Bible (Public Domain). Scripture quotations marked (NIV) are taken from the Holy Bible, New International Version®, NIV®. Copyright © 1973, 1978, 1984 by Biblica, Inc.™ Used by permission of Zondervan. All rights reserved worldwide. http://www.zondervan.com. Scripture quotations marked "NKJV" are taken from the New King James Version. Copyright © 1982 by Thomas Nelson, Inc. Used by permission. All rights reserved. Bible text from the New King James Version® is not to be reproduced in copies or otherwise by any means except as permitted in writing by Thomas Nelson, Inc., Attn: Bible Rights and Permissions, P.O. Box 141000, Nashville, TN 37214-1000. http://www.nelsonbibles.com/

ISBN 978-1-947741-10-2

Recommendations

I applaud another publication by Apostle Aaron B. Claxton! Having been a student in many of his university level classes, as well as an avid reader of his many books, I highly recommend reading this book, "Unveiling the Truth about the War in the Womb." Professor Claxton is not only an expert scholar on Biblical matters, but is also an exceptional teacher. His working knowledge of scripture is indeed impressive and is equal to, or exceeds, any modern day expert on critical biblical interpretation. But, professor Claxton's true blessing is in his unique ability to break down very complex and detailed doctrine into an easily understandable, readable, and comprehensible format. Dr. Claxton talks the talk, but more importantly walks the walk of a true spiritual father and Christian leader to many, including myself. If you want to learn, understand, and gain insight into the modern day issues of Israel and the Middle East from an authentic biblical expert, Apostle Claxton's book, "Unveiling the Truth about the War in the Womb," is indeed a must read.

– Deacon Anthony Allen IV MS, Counselor

Apostle Aaron Claxton has done it again. The Lord has gifted him with the ability to hear divine revelation and insight on scriptural passages that have more than a surface interpretation. As you read "Understanding the War in the

Womb," expect to receive wisdom and spiritual perception, which will assist you with understanding the historical and contemporary conflicts in the Middle East. Apostle Claxton's approach to the debates surrounding the nation of Israel is neither political nor personal, but a biblical context and point of reference. Enjoy learning and applying God's prophetic tapestry for His Jewish people and His Church.

TABLE OF CONTENTS

Chapter One
War in the Womb
1

Chapter Two
The Wild Donkey Man
5

Chapter Three
Esau's Choice
9

Chapter Four
Mohammed's Religion, the Religion of the Arabs and the Sword, is Esau's Religion
11

Chapter Five
Mohammed's Religion, the Religion of the Arabs, Becomes Esau's Religion and People
17

Chapter Six
Leaning Toward the End
23

Chapter Seven
God Spoils Esau as Recorded by Obadiah
27

Chapter One
War in the Womb

The story of "War in the Womb" is found in Genesis 25:20-26. It will affect the history of the world and God Himself will end the Middle East Conflict. The story reads thusly:

> "Isaac was forty years old when he took Rebekah as his wife, the daughter of Bethuel, the Syrian of Padam aram, the sister of Laban the Syrian."

In Genesis chapter eleven we find that from the sons of Shem, the youngest son of Noah, came Eber, the father of the Hebrews, and Aram the father of the Syrians. So that the Hebrews and

Syrians are related by blood, although they are at odds today and of different religions, Judaism and Islam. Since they were related by blood, Isaac could send Jacob to Rebekah's people to take a wife. Genesis 28:1-4 says, "Then Isaac called Jacob and blessed him, and charged him, and said to him: 'You shall not take a wife from the daughters of Canaan. Arise, go to Padan-aram, to the house of Bethuel your mother's father; and take yourself a wife from there of the daughters of Laban your mother's brother. And Isaac prayed a prayer of blessing on Jacob decreeing the blessing of Abraham upon him and his descendants "that you may inherit the land in which you are a stranger, which God gave to Abraham" (Gen 28:1-4).

Now back to the "War in the Womb" (Genesis 25:21-26):

"Now Isaac pleaded with the Lord for his wife, because she was barren; and Rebekah his wife conceived. (Isaac was forty years old at the time) "But the children struggled together within her; and she said, 'If it is well, why am I like this?' So she went to inquire of the Lord. And the Lord said to her: "Two nations are in your womb; two peoples shall be separated from your body; one people shall be stronger than the other, and the older shall serve the younger.

So when her days were fulfilled for her to give birth, indeed there were twins in her womb. And

Chapter One - War in the Womb

the first came out red. He was like a hairy garment all over; so they called his name Esau (hairy). Afterward his brother came out, and took hold of Esau's heel; so his name was called Jacob (Supplanter or deceitful, one who takes the heel). So the boys grew. And Esau was a skillful hunter, a man of the field; but Jacob was a mild man, dwelling in tents. And Isaac loved Esau because he ate his game, but Rebekah loved Jacob" (Genesis 25:20-28).

You will notice from the Bible story above that there were two nations at war or struggling within Rebekah's womb. As a matter of fact, the Apostle Paul touches on this subject in Romans 9:6-14, while dealing with the subject of <u>selection and non-selection</u> among Abraham's seed. Paul wrote, *"But it is not that the word of God has taken no effect. For they are not all Israel who are of Israel. Nor are they all children because they are the seed of Abraham; <u>but in Isaac your seed shall be called</u>. That is, those who are the children of the flesh (Ishmael), these are not the children of God; the children of the promise (Isaac) are counted as the seed (of the Covenant)…* "*And not only this, but when Rebecca also had conceived by one man, even by our father Isaac (for the children not yet being born, not having done any good or evil, that the purpose of God according to election (choice) might stand, not of works but of Him who calls) it was said to her, the older shall serve the younger.*

As it is written, 'Jacob have I loved, but Esau I have hated!' What shall we say then? Is there unrighteousness with God? Certainly not!" Through God's foreknowledge He saw what Esau would become, <u>a defector!</u> and turn his back on God, and connect with the Arab side of the family.

When Paul wrote in Romans 9:13, "As it is written, 'Jacob have I loved but Esau have I hated,' Paul was quoting from the Prophet Malachi who said, "The burden of the word of the Lord to Israel by Malachi."

> "I have loved you," says the Lord, Yet you say, 'In what way have you loved us? Was not Esau Jacob's brother?' says the Lord. 'Yet Jacob have I loved; but Esau have I hated, and laid waste his mountains and his heritage for the jackals of the wilderness" (Malachi 1:1-3).

In order to better understand why God hated Esau from the womb, we need to look back at one of Esau's older relatives (his uncle) Ishmael who was an enemy of God with whom Esau became connected by marriage.

Chapter Two
The Wild Donkey Man[1]

In Genesis Chapter Sixteen we read about Hagar's flight from Sarai and her encounter with the Angel of the Lord.

"And Sarai saith unto Abram, 'My violence is for thee; I have given my handmaid into thy bosom and she seeth that she hath conceived, and her mistress is lightly esteemed in her eyes; Jehovah doth judge between me and thee! And Abram saith unto Sarai, 'Lo thine handmaid is in

---

[1] Most of our quotes are from Young's Literal Translation of the Holy Bible.

thine hand, do to her that is good in thine eyes'! And Sarai afflicted her, and she fleeth from her presence."

"And a messenger of Jehovah (the Angel of the Lord, or Jesus in the Old Testament) findeth her by the fountains or water in the wilderness, by the fountain in the way to Shur, and be saith, 'Hagar, Sarai's handmaid, whence hast thou come, and whither dost thou go? 'And she saith, 'from the presence of Sarai, my mistress, I am fleeing!

"And a messenger of Jehovah saith to her, 'Turn back unto thy mistress, and humble thyself under her hands; and the messenger of Jehovah saith unto her 'Multiplying I multiply thy seed, and it is not numbered from multitude; and the messenger of Jehovah saith to her, 'Behold thou art conceiving, and bearing a son, and hast called his name Ishmael, for Jehovah hath hearkened unto thine affliction; and he is a wild-ass man, his hand against every one, any everyone's hand against him-and before the face of all his brethren he dwelleth…And Hagar beareth to Abram a son; and Abram calleth the name of his son, whom Hagar hath borne, Ishmael."

Verse 12 above reads a bit differently in the NIV Bible.

Chapter Two - The Wild Donkey Man

Verse 12 in the NIV Version of the Bible reads: "He will be <u>a wild donkey of a man; his hand will be against everyone and everyone's hand against him</u>, and <u>he will live in hostility toward all his brothers.</u>"

Let us state clearly that Ishmael is the first <u>Arab</u> on <u>earth</u> – a cross between Hebrew and Egyptian (African) blood. That is, the offspring of Abram and Hagar.

From the voluminous book entitled, "GOD'S WAR ON TERROR, Islam, Prophecy AND THE BIBLE" by Walid Shoebat with Joel Richardson pp. 316-317 under the heading of <u>Arabization or ARABIZM</u> they say:

> "The other meaning of the riddle in this verse (Daniel 2:41) needs to be noted; the underlined words "mixed" and "combined" are actually the same words translated differently from Aramaic, the original language of the Book of Daniel. The word is actually "Arabs."
>
> <u>Strong's Concordance</u> confirms this:
>
> "Marrab (Ar-ab;' from"arab '(6150) in the figurative sense of sterility; Arab (i.e.Arabia), a country East of Palestine: Arabia." "or mereb (I Kings 10:15) with the article prefix, (eh'-reb]; from "arab' (6148); the web (or transverse threads of a cloth); also a mixture, (or mongrel

race); --Arabia, mingled people, mixed (multitude), woof."

And thus this passage can read:

"And just as you saw the iron mixed with baked clay, so the people will be mixed (Arabized) with the seed of men (through intermarriage) and not remain united, any more than iron does not mix with clay…"

Ibn Ezra is troubled by the absence of the kingdom of Ishmael, viz the Arabs and the Turks who were very powerful in his time. He therefore concludes that the …fourth kingdom (in Daniel 2) is the kingdom of Ishmael. "God's War on Terror" page 317.

Let's go back and pick up the threads of truth to help our understanding. The book of Daniel was written originally in Aramaic. Remember we mentioned Aram, the father of the Syrians, the cousins of the Israelites? Well, Aramaic also called Syriac, is one of the dialects of the Hebrew. It is the dialect that Jesus spoke while here on earth – the Hebrew of the common people! Syriac is one of the languages in which the Old Testament Bible is written, along with Hebrew and Greek.

Chapter Three
Esau's Choice

Esau was begged by His parents not to marry any of the Hittite (Canaanite) women where they (the Israelites) dwelled. Esau chose the Arab side of His family by marrying his first cousin Mahalath, the daughter of his Uncle Ishmael.

Let's pick up the story from the Bible in Genesis 28:6-9!

"Now Esau learned that Isaac had blessed Jacob and sent him to Padan-aram to take a wife from there, and that when he blessed him he commanded him, 'Do not marry a Canaanite woman,' and that Jacob had obeyed his father and mother and had gone to Padan-aram. Esau then realized how displeasing the Canaanite women were to his father Isaac; so he went to Ishmael (the father of the Arabs) and married Mahalath….and daughter of Ishmael, son of Abraham, in addition to the wives he already had, Esau married Mahalath out of anger and spite."

I believe Esau was moved by an evil spirit to defect from God and go the way of God's chief adversaries, who were of the devil. Muslims, in later years, Mohammed their founder is the direct descendant of Ishmael, "the wild donkey man" who would one day seek to rule the world by the force of the sword.

Once Esau realized he had lost his birthright and firstborn blessing to Jacob his twin brother, as well as the favor of his parents, he bacame wroth, "And Esau hated Jacob, because of the blessing with which his father blessed him and Esau saith in his heart, "the days of mourning for my father draw near, and I slay my brother, Jacob'" (Genesis 27:41).

Chapter Four
Mohammed's Religion, the Religion of the Arabs and the Sword, is Esau's Religion

The two nations at war in Rebekah's womb were Israel and Arabia. Before them were the two nations of Isaac and Ishmael. Abraham's religion of Judaism began in 2,000 B.C. with The Covenant of Circumcision. We find this Covenant of God with Abraham in Genesis 17:1-27.

The word of God says,

"When Abraham was ninety-nine years old, the Lord appeared to him and said, 'I am God Almighty; (El Shaddai), walk before me and be blameless. I will confirm my covenant between me and you and will greatly increase your numbers! Abram fell face down, and God said to him, 'As for me this is my covenant with you: You will be the father of many nations. No longer will you be called Abram; your name will be Abraham, for I have made you a father of many nations. I will make you very fruitful; I will make nations of you, and kings will come from you. I will establish my covenant between me and you and your descendants after you; and I will be their God!"

"Then God said to Abraham; 'As for you, you must keep my covenant, you and your descendants after you for the generations to come. This is my covenant with you and your descendants after you, the covenant you are to keep: Every male among you shall be circumcised. You are to undergo circumcision and it will be a sign between me and you. For the generations to come every male among you who is eight days old must be circumcised, including those born in your household or bought with money from a foreigner-those who are not your offspring...they must be circumcised. My covenant in your flesh is to be an everlasting covenant. Any uncircumcised male, who has not been circumcised in the flesh

Chapter Four - Mohammed's Religion, the Religion of the Arabs and the Sword, is Esau's Religion

will be cut off from his people; he has broken my covenant.'

"God also said to Abraham,' As for Sarai your wife, you are no longer to call her Sarai; her name will be Sarah. I will bless her and will surely give you a son by her. I will bless her so that she will be the mother of nations, kings of people will come from her.'"

Having just noted in the passages above that "The Covenant of Circumcision" was given by God to Abraham and his descendants through Isaac and Jacob – not Ishmael or Esau!

On page 237 of Walid Shobat's book, "God's War On Terror, Islam, Prophecy, And The Bible" we read:

"IRAN, here is Elam and all her multitude round her grave, all of them slain, fallen by the sword, which are gone down uncircumcised into the nether parts of the earth, which caused their terror in the land of the living; yet they have borne their shame with them that go down to the pit (Ezekiel 32:24). Elam encompasses the region of modern day Iran and perhaps regions of Afghanistan. Again we see that they also will, "go down to the pit" with the Antichrist...'

"We know that circumcision is the mark of God's covenant with Abraham and Isaac.

(Genesis 17:19) Because all male members of the household were circumcised (Genesis 17:12-13), Ishmael was therefore circumcised-even though the covenant was not made with him."

BUT MUSLIMS ARE CIRCUMCISED

"And it may also be noted that some rabbinic interpreters also do not see this verse (Ezekiel 44:7) as ruling out Muslims; Technically Orthodox Jews do not consider Muslim circumcision to be complete circumcision as Muslims only remove the prepuce or outer foreskin, while the Jews also remove the pariah or the inner foreskin."

Now back to Abraham and Sarah in Genesis 17:17:

"Abraham fell face down, he laughed and said to himself, 'Will a son be born to a man hundred years old? Will Sarah bear a child at the age of ninety?' And Abraham said to God 'O that Ishmael may live before thee' (Young's Literal Translation) and God saith, 'Sarah thy wife is certainly bearing a son to thee, and thou hast called his name Isaac, I have established my covenant with him, (this, the Arab-Muslims don't accept) for a covenant age-enduring, to his

Chapter Four - Mohammed's Religion, the Religion of the Arabs and the Sword, is Esau's Religion

seed after him. As to Ishmael, I have heard thee; lo, I have blessed him, and made him fruitful and multiplied him, very exceedingly; twelve princes doth he beget, and I have made him a great nation; and my covenant I establish with Isaac whom Sarah doth bear to thee (a year later) at this appointed time in the next year; and He finished speaking with, and God (The Angel of The LORD) goeth up from Abraham."

Chapter Five
Mohammed's Religion, the Religion of the Arabs, Becomes Esau's Religion and People

The Religion of Mohammed was birthed many centuries after Esau's death (in the Seventh Century A.D.-610-622 A.D.), and Esau was elevated above Ishmael in the Arabian scheme of things by God Himself.

Let us examine the words of Isaac's blessing spoken over Esau.

"And Esau saith unto his father, 'One blessing hast thou my father? Bless me, me also, O my father; 'And Esau lifteth up his voice and weepeth."

"And Isaac his father answereth and saith unto him, 'Lo the <u>fatness of the earth is thy dwelling</u>, (I believe that to be the rich oil fields of Saudi Arabia today) and the dew of the heavens from above; <u>and by the sword dost thou live</u> (I believe this to be the Arabs we know throughout world history) and thy brother dost thou serve; and it hath come to pass when thou rulest that thou hast broken his yoke from off thy neck. "And Esau hateth Jacob, because of the blessing with which his faher blessed him, and Esau saith in his heart, 'The days of mourning for my father draw near, and I slay Jacob my brother'.

"And the words of Esau her elder son are declared to Rebekah, and she sendeth and calleth Jacob her younger son, and saith unto him, 'Lo, Esau thy broher is conforting himself in regard to thee-to slay thee; and now, my son, hearken to my voice, and rise, flee for thyself unto Laban , my brother, to Haran (Padan-aram), and when thou hast dwelt with him some days, (twenty years) till thy brother's fury turn back, till thy brother's anger turn back from thee, and he hath forgotten that which thou hast done to him, and

Chapter Five - Mohammed's Religion, the Religion of the Arabs, Becomes Esau's Religion and People

I have sent and taken thee from thence; Why am I bereaved even of you both the same day?'... "And Isaac sendeth away Jacob, and he goeth to Padan-aram unto, Laban, son of Bethuel the Aramaen, (the Syrian) brother of Rebekah, mother of Jacob and Esau."

God called Abram out of Ur of the Chaldees (Iraq) when he was an idol worshipper – a worshipper of many false gods. The Lord (Yahweh) revealed Himself to Abram as the one and only true and Living God, (creator of the heavens and the earth). This true God conversed with and answered Abram as a living, intelligent, and holy Being. Abram's previous "gods" did not do so. Islam would know nothing of a monotheistic God, except they read about Him in the ancient Holy Scriptures of the Bible! The Muslims came forth in the 7th century A.D., and borrowed ideas from the 2000 year old Holy Bible and twisted its message. Muslims are famous for lying and twisting the truth. Satan the devil is their true father!

It was a satanic, demonic spirit that appeared to Muhammed as an "angel" while he was fasting in a cave outside of Mecca, and practically squeezed the breath out of him three times and commanded him to recite the Muslim Creed known as the Shahadatan which says: "there is no God but Allah, and Mohammed is his messenger."

God the Father and Jesus Christ His Son both hate the religion of Islam. It is the only religion on earth that has sought to supplant and replace the Judeo-Christian faith as the one true faith for all mankind. Islam has muscled its way into world history and world religions. They are deceivers as their father the devil is the arch deceiver in the world!

The words of Jesus to backslidden Jews in St. John 8:42-44 are applicable to Muslims today.

> "Jesus said to them 'If God were your Father, you would love me, for I came from God and now am here. I have not come on my own; but he sent me. Why is my language not clear to you? Because you are unable to hear what I say. You belong to your father, the devil, and you want to carry out your father's desire. He was a murderer from the beginning, not holding to the truth, for there is no truth in him. When he lies, he speaks his native language, for he is a liar and the father of lies." Revelation 20:7 says: "When the thousand years are over, Satan will be released from his prison and will go out to deceive the nations in the four corners of the earth..."

As we allow our minds to go back to Abram and Hagar, Hagar knew full well that Ishmael was the firstborn of Abram and "should" have received the firstborn blessing and inheritance from his father Abram. However, God himself said "No! My covenant I will establish with Isaac" (Genesis 17:21). I find that Arabs are stubborn people and will not take no for an answer! They (deceived by Satan) believe in their hearts that the

Chapter Five - Mohammed's Religion, the Religion of the Arabs, Becomes Esau's Religion and People

covenant of God with Abraham belongs to them – despite what is stated in the Bible at least five times! The covenant and the promises of God, and especially <u>the Holy Land, belong to Israel</u> – Abraham, Isaac and Jacob (Israel) – not Ishmael and Esau! The Arabs seem to feel that as long as they keep repeating their false claims against Israel that the world will (and is) siding with them that Israel is an <u>occupant</u> of the Holy Land, <u>not owners</u>!

Arabs have always claimed the right of the firstborn son, Esau, over Jacob the second born son of Isaac and Rebekah. In the very scheme of things, Arabs have always claimed and boasted in their firstborn position of Esau over Jacob.

Over the weekend of May 20-21 we observed on T.V. the great pomp and circumstance of Saudi Arabia in Mecca, the birthplace of Islam, and fifty Arab nations who gathered there to greet and meet with our new President, Donald Trump. They cut military deals with the U.S. worth 110 billion dollars. They are the offspring of Abram and Hagar, and Abraham and Keturah, <u>a black Arabian maiden</u> whom Abraham married after Sarah's death. Abraham had six sons by Keturah and many years later Moses fled from Egypt and wound up in Midian, one of the offspring of Abraham and Keturah. There were numerous black Arabs, as well as, black Africans who met with President Trump. In Dubai, a very rich and modern city are many dark Arabians. They are offspring of Abraham and Keturah.

Chapter Six
Leaning Toward the End

God in His awesome foreknowledge foresaw the end of the matter of the struggle between Esau and Jacob, while they (the twins) were in the womb. The Lord records the end of the struggle between the brothers in the one Chapter prophecy of Obadiah. But before we look at the end of the matter, let us look back at the beginning when God warned Israel through Moses of the consequences of their forsaking Him and going after other gods.

Let us read the warning God gave the children of Israel in Deuteronomy 4:25-31:

"After you have had children and grandchildren and have lived in the land a longtime-if you then become corrupt and make any kind of idol, doing evil in the eyes of the Lord your God and provoking him to anger: I call heaven and earth as witnesses against you this day that you will quickly perish from the land that you are crossing the Jordan to possess.

"You will not live there long but will certainly be destroyed. <u>The Lord will scatter you among the peoples</u>, and only a few of you will survive among the nations to worship man-made gods of wood and stone, which cannot see or hear or eat or smell. But if from there you seek the LORD your God, you will find him if you look for him with all your heart and with all your soul. When you are in distress and all these things have happened to you, then <u>in the later days you will return</u> to the <u>LORD your God and obey him</u>. For the LORD your God is a merciful God; <u>he will not abandon or destroy you or forget the covenant with your forefathers, which was confirmed by oath-including the promise of the Holy Land</u>."

The scene above took place around 1400 B.C. during Moses ministry. Some 700 years later (721 B.C.), after the prophets had pleaded and warned Israel about her idolatry, the <u>10</u>

Chapter Six - Leaning Toward the End

<u>Northern tribes of Israel were scattered among several nations</u> by the Assyrians, fulfilling God's warnings to them through Moses, some 700 years before. Then in 597-582 B.C. Judah, <u>the southern tribe fell to Nebuchadnezzar of Babylon. The Jews became captives of Babylon for 70 years</u>, according to the prophecy of Jeremiah 29:10.

Then during the ministry of Jesus the Messiah (30 A.D. to 33 A.D.), <u>he prophesied the Jews and Israelites' third and final expulsion from the holy land because of the Jews' disobedience to the voice of God</u>. Matthew 24:1-2 records the following:

> "Jesus left the temple and was walking away when his disciples came up to him to call his attention to its building. 'Do you see all these things?' he asked. 'I tell you the truth, not one stone, not one stone here will be left on another; everyone will be thrown down.'"

Jesus is here prophesying <u>the destruction of Jerusalem by Titus the Roman general and his armies in 70 A.D.</u>

The Romans, The Muslims, the Christian Crusaders and the British, to name a few all invaded and occupied the Holy Land. For centuries both Jewish and Arab remnants remained in the holy land.

Chapter Seven
God Spoils Esau as Recorded by Obadiah

The Book of OBADIAH

A struggle that began in the womb between twin brothers, Esau and Jacob, eventuated in a struggle between their respective decendants, the Edomites (the Esauites) and the Israelites. For the Edomites' stubborn refusal to aid Israel, first during the time of wilderness wandering (numbers 20:14-21) and later during a time of invasion, they are roundly condemned by Obadiah. This little-known prophet describes their crimes, tries their case, and pronounces their judgement: total destruction (on Esau).

The Hebrew name Obadiah means "Worshipper of Yahweh" or "servant of Yahweh" (excerpts from the New King James

Bible). Now we go to the New International Version of the Holy Bible.

"The vision of Obadiah. This is what the sovereign LORD says about Edom – 'We have heard a message from the LORD: an enemy was sent to the nation to say, 'Rise and let us go against her for battle'

'See, I will make you small among the nations, you will be utterly despised.

The pride in your heart has deceived you, (*Remember Esau or Edom, became the founder and chief exponent of Islam!*) you will live in clefts of the rocks and make your home on the heights, you who say to yourself, 'Who can bring me down to the ground?'

Though you soar like the eagle and make your nest among the stars, from there I will bring you down,' declares the LORD.

(Hey, those words above sound like the words of Lucifer recorded in Isaiah 14:12-15:

"How you have fallen from heaven, O morning star, son of the dawn! (Same name as Allah) You have been cast down to the earth, you who once laid low the nations! You said in your heart,

Chapter Seven - God Spoils Esau as Recorded by Obadiah

'I will ascend to heaven; (Mohammed was supposedly assumed into heaven) I will raise my throne above the stars of God; 'I will sit enthroned on the mount of assembly, on the utmost heights of the sacred mountain. 'I will ascend to the tops of the clouds;
'I will make myself like the most High.' "But you are brought down to the grave, to the depths of the pit.

'If thieves came to you, if robbers in the night - Oh, what a disaster awaits you - would they not steal only as much as they wanted? If grape pickers came to you, would they not leave a few grapes?

But how Esau will be ransacked, his hidden treasures pillaged!

All your allies will force you to the border; your friends will deceive and overpower you; those who eat your bread will set a trap for you, but you will not detect it.

"In that day" declares the LORD, 'Will I not destroy the wise men of Edom, men of understanding in the mountains of ESAU?

Your Warriors, O Teman, (Esau's grandson) will be terrified, and everyone in Esau's mountains will be cut down in the slaughter.

Because of the violence against your brother Jacob, you will be covered with shame; 'You will be destroyed forever.

On the day you stood aloof while strangers carried off his wealth and foreigners entered his gates and cast lots for Jerusalem, You were like one of them.

You should not look down on your brother in the day of his misfortune, nor rejoice over the people of Judah in the day of their destruction, nor boast so much in the day of their trouble.

You should not march through the gates of my people in the day of their disaster, nor look down on them in their calamity in the day of their disaster, nor seize their wealth in the day of their disaster.

'You should not wait at the crossroads to cut down their fugitives, nor hand over their survivors in the day of their trouble.

"The day of the LORD is near for all nations. As you have done, it will be done to you, Your deeds will return upon your own head.

Just as you drank on my holy hill, so all nations will drink continually; they will drink and drink and be as though and be as if they had never been.

Chapter Seven - God Spoils Esau as Recorded by Obadiah

"But on Mount Zion will be deliverance; it will be holy, and the house of Jacob will possess its inheritance (The Holy Land).

The house of Jacob will be a fire and the house of Joseph a flame; the house of Esau will be stubble, and they will set it (the house of Esau) on fire and consume it. There will be no survivors from the house of Esau. "The LORD has spoken…"

Deliverers will go up to Mount Zion to govern the mountains Of Esau. "And the kingdom will be the Lord's."

And thus you have heard and seen the end of the story of how the Middle East conflict will be resolved shortly. You have seen and heard the end of the mystery of the "War in the Womb." God has given us the end of the story, Amen!

About the Author

Dr. Aaron B. Claxton has been in Christ for nearly 60 years and has preached the Gospel for nearly 60 years.

Dr. Claxton is the father of seven children, which initially and graciously began with his precious firstborn daughter, Gayle.

He has been married to his lovely wife, Deborah, for 60 years. They are the proud parents of six children (four boys and two girls), all have been called into the five-fold ministry. The Claxtons are also blessed with a host of grandchildren and great grandchildren.

Dr. Claxton's academic background includes earned degrees from Morgan State University, from the Mount Royal College of the Bible and from St. Mary's Semi-nary and University, where he pursued the academics for the Doctor of Ministry degree. He completed that degree in 1996 at the Family Bible Seminary.

Dr. Claxton has been awarded two honorary Doctorate degrees from Christian International University. They are the Doctor of Divinity and the Doctor of Laws degrees. He received his PhD degree in Biblical Studies from Family Bible Seminary in May 2003.

In addition to this prolific masterpiece, Dr. Claxton has authored over thirty (30) books of which nine (9) others are published (in addition to this one):

1 – "God's Plan for the Sons of Ham – a future and a

hope"
2 – "The Biblical View of the Rapture and the Second Coming"
3 – "Farrakhan, Islam and Jesus the Messiah"
4 – "The Blessing of the Lord is Upon the Tither"
5 – "First Fruits the Missing Offering"
6 – "Possessing Our Earthly Inheritance Now!"
7 – "Caught Up to Meet Him"
8 – "Understanding the Root, the Causes and the Remedy of the Middle East Conflict"
9 – "ISIS – The Church's Wake Up Call"

Apostle Claxton, along with his wife, Deborah, founded and pastored the New Creation Christian Church in Baltimore, Maryland for twenty-three years. He has taught at three Bible Colleges and is well traveled, having preached the Gospel across America and in sixteen nations around the world.

Dr. Claxton stands in the offices of Apostle and Bishop, formally overseeing one hundred plus churches in the U.S., and in East and West Africa, and is presently being established in a global, apostolic ministry, along with his wife, Deborah, in her apostolic ministry. His oldest son, Apostle Aaron Bryan Claxton, along with his wife, Sheila, now pastor the headquarters church in Baltimore, which Dr. Claxton founded in 1968.

www.ingramcontent.com/pod-product-compliance
Lightning Source LLC
Chambersburg PA
CBHW071549080526
44588CB00011B/1840